Y0-AZG-584

One Spirit:

A Creation Story for the 21st Century.

One Spirit

A Creation Story for the 21st Century.

By Jean Latz Griffin

Illustrated by Jane Gaunt

CyberINK
Arlington Heights, IL

Copyright © 2006 by Jean Latz Griffin
All rights reserved. Printed in the United States of America.

First edition, 2006
No part of this book may be used or reproduced in any manner
whatsoever without written permission except in the case of
brief quotations embodied in critical articles and reviews. For information,
contact publisher CyberINK, 621 N. Belmont Ave., Arlington Hts., IL 60004.

Publisher's Cataloging-in-Publication
(Provided by Quality Books, Inc.)

Griffin, Jean Latz.
   One Spirit : a creation story for the 21st century /
by Jean Latz Griffin ; illustrated by Jane Gaunt.
   p. cm.
   LCCN 2005910221
   ISBN 0976861038

   1. Creation--Pictorial works. 2. Evolution--
Religious aspects--Pictorial works. 3. Consciousness--
Pictorial works.   I. Gaunt, Jane, ill. II. Title.

BL227.G75 2006   213
                        QBI06-600003

Designed by CyberINK

All images © 2006 Jane Gaunt

This book is lovingly dedicated to our mothers.

Helene Monica Bradshaw Latz
1902 - 1997

Mary Elise Doudna Gaunt
1923 - 1998

Design by CyberINK

Once, long ago...

...there was
One Spirit.

It was all that existed.

It had always existed.

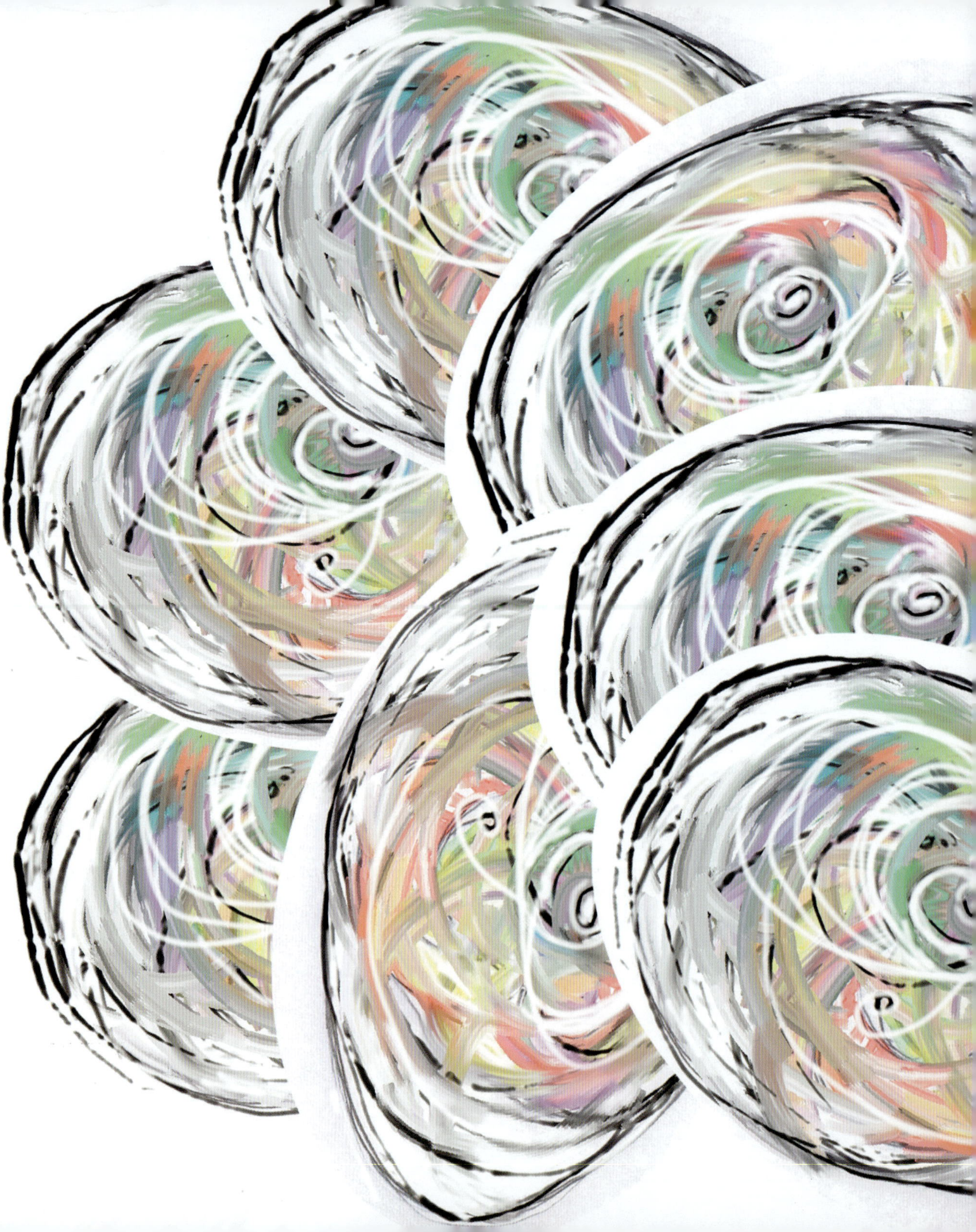

And One Spirit was bored.

Always turning on itself.

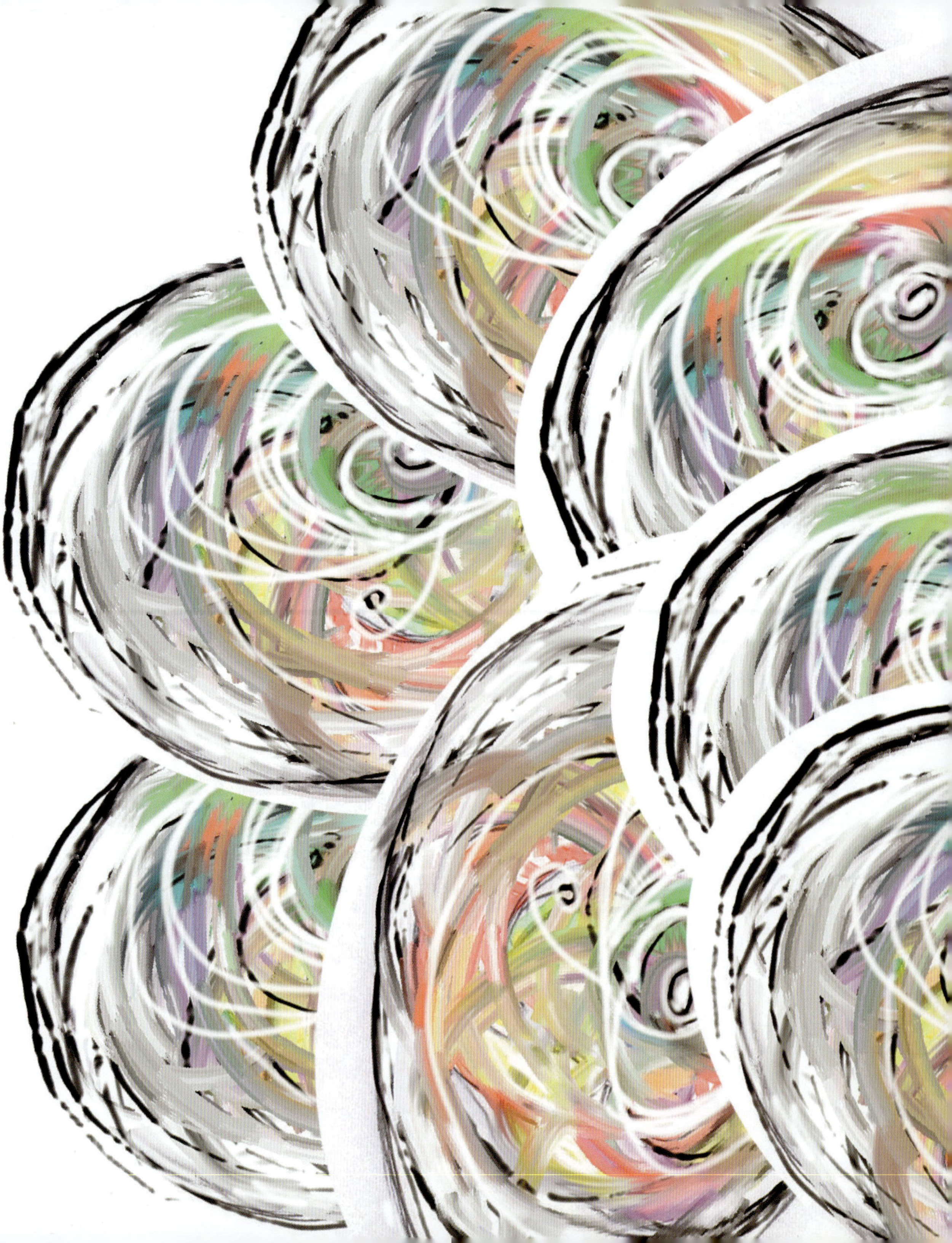

Spinning in an egg-shaped sphere.

But bored by sameness.

So

One Spirit

decided

to

explode.

To become other than a single sphere.

Gaunt

To differentiate itself, like a growing embryo...

... into

light,

energy,

matter.

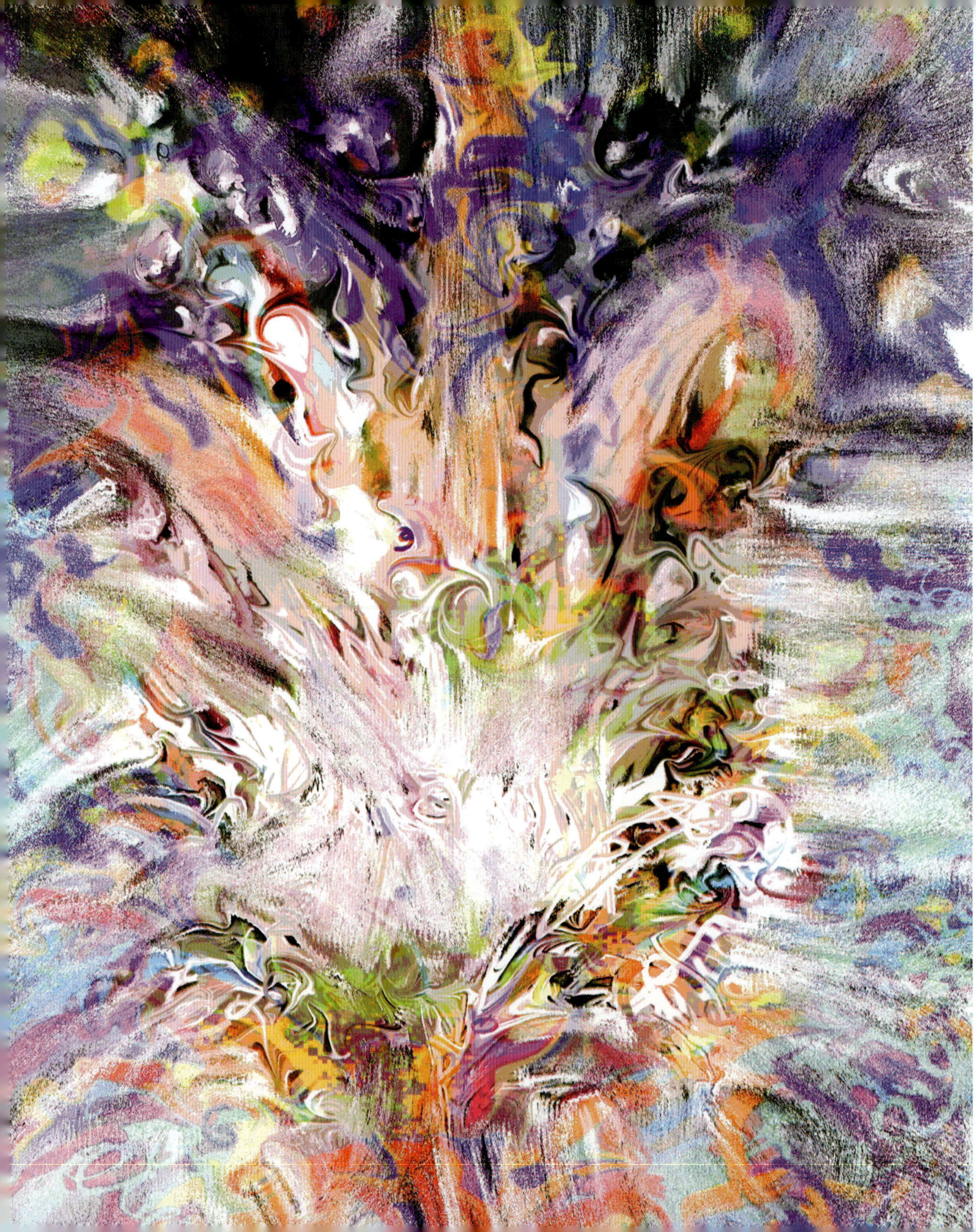

And then living beings,

tiny at first,

then larger...

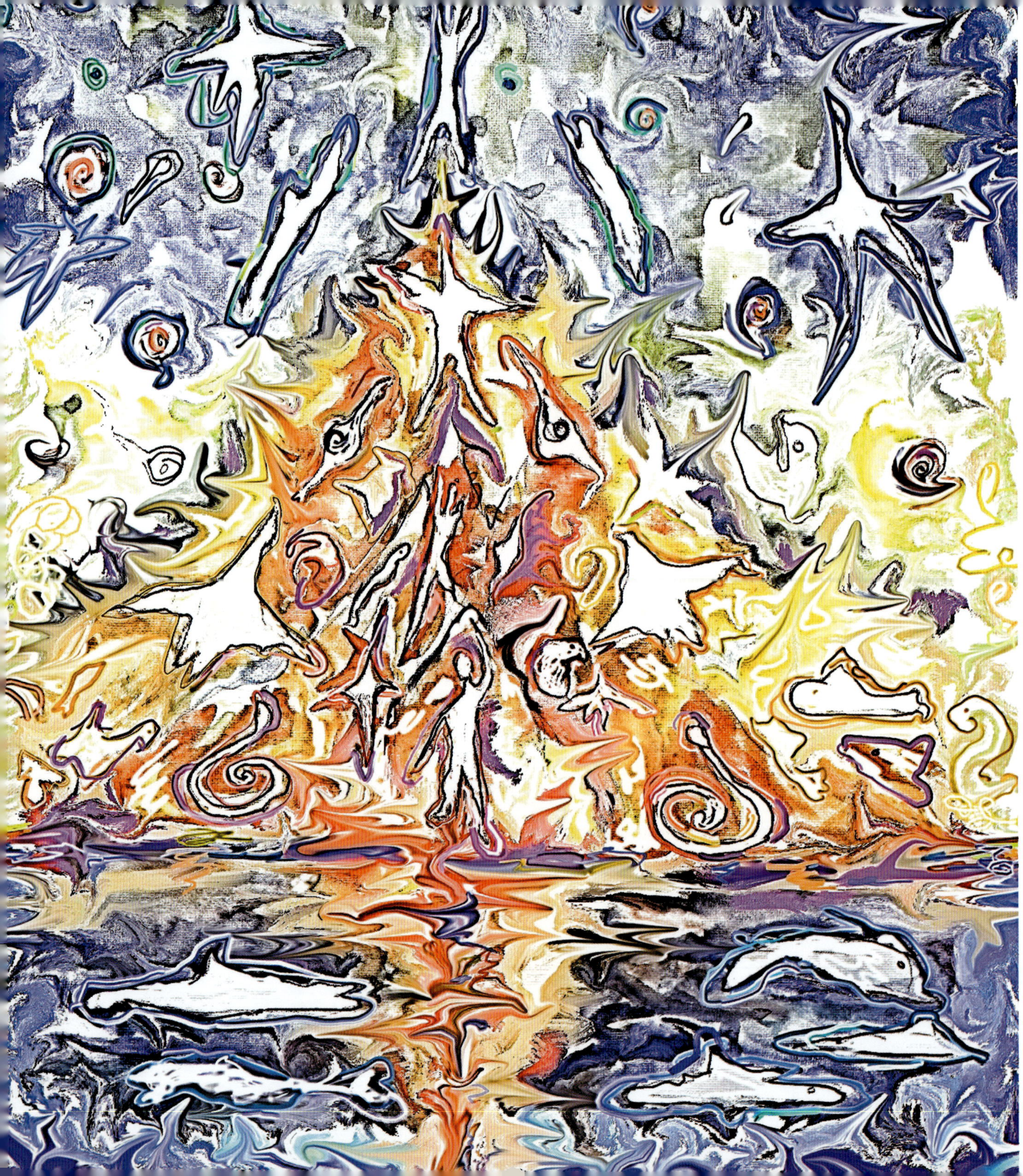

moving

swimming

flying

running...

Thinking....

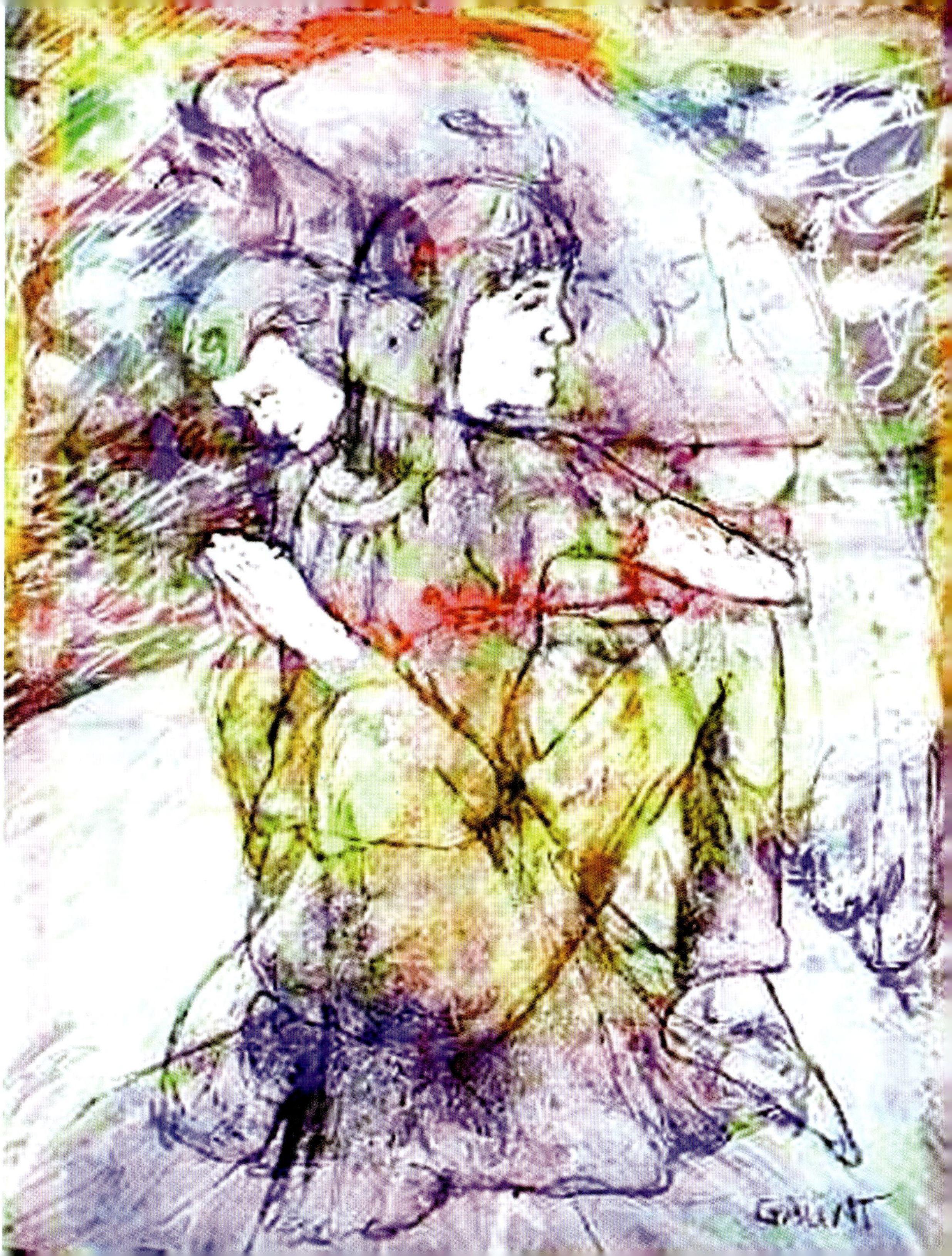
GALLANT

loving.

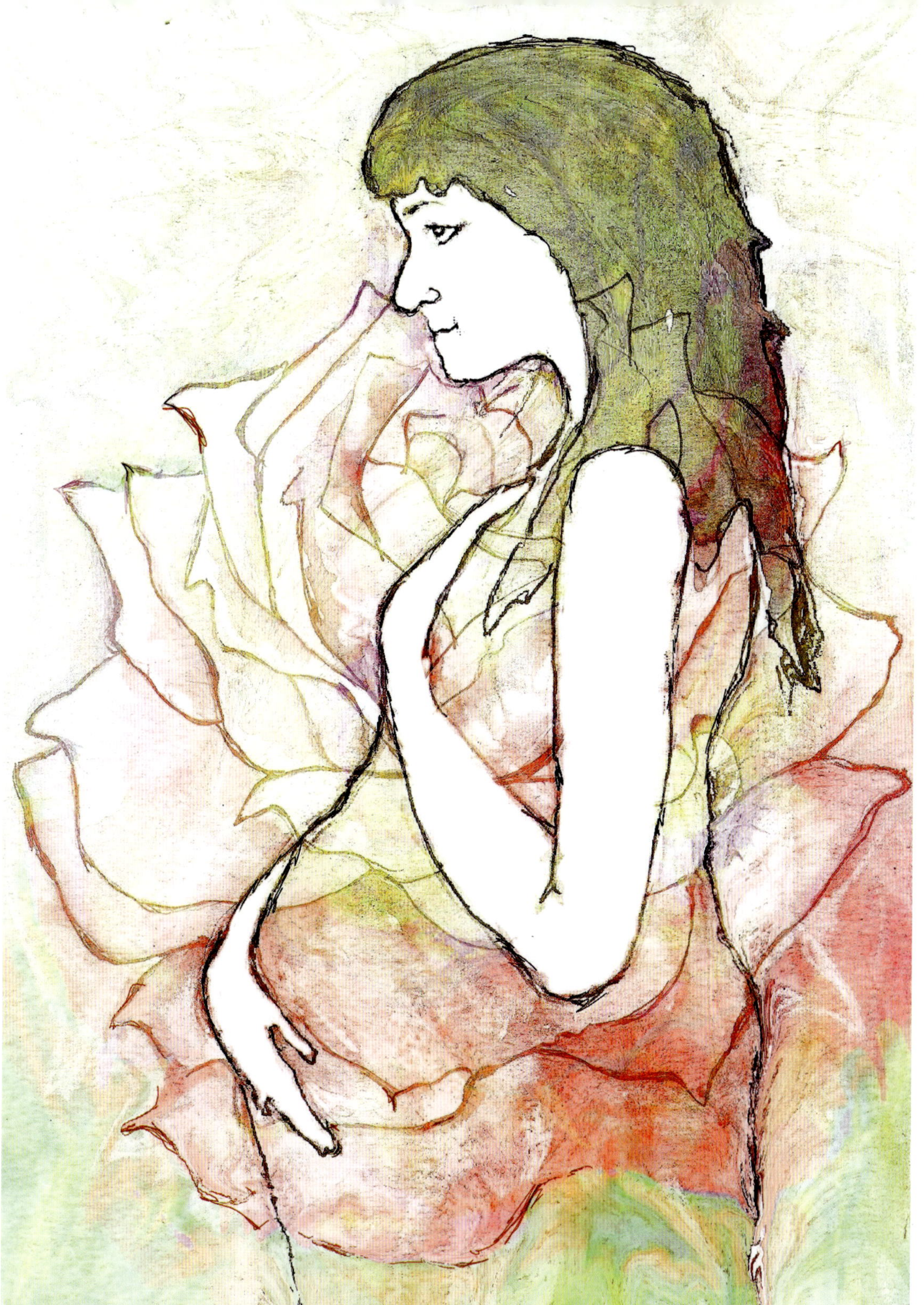

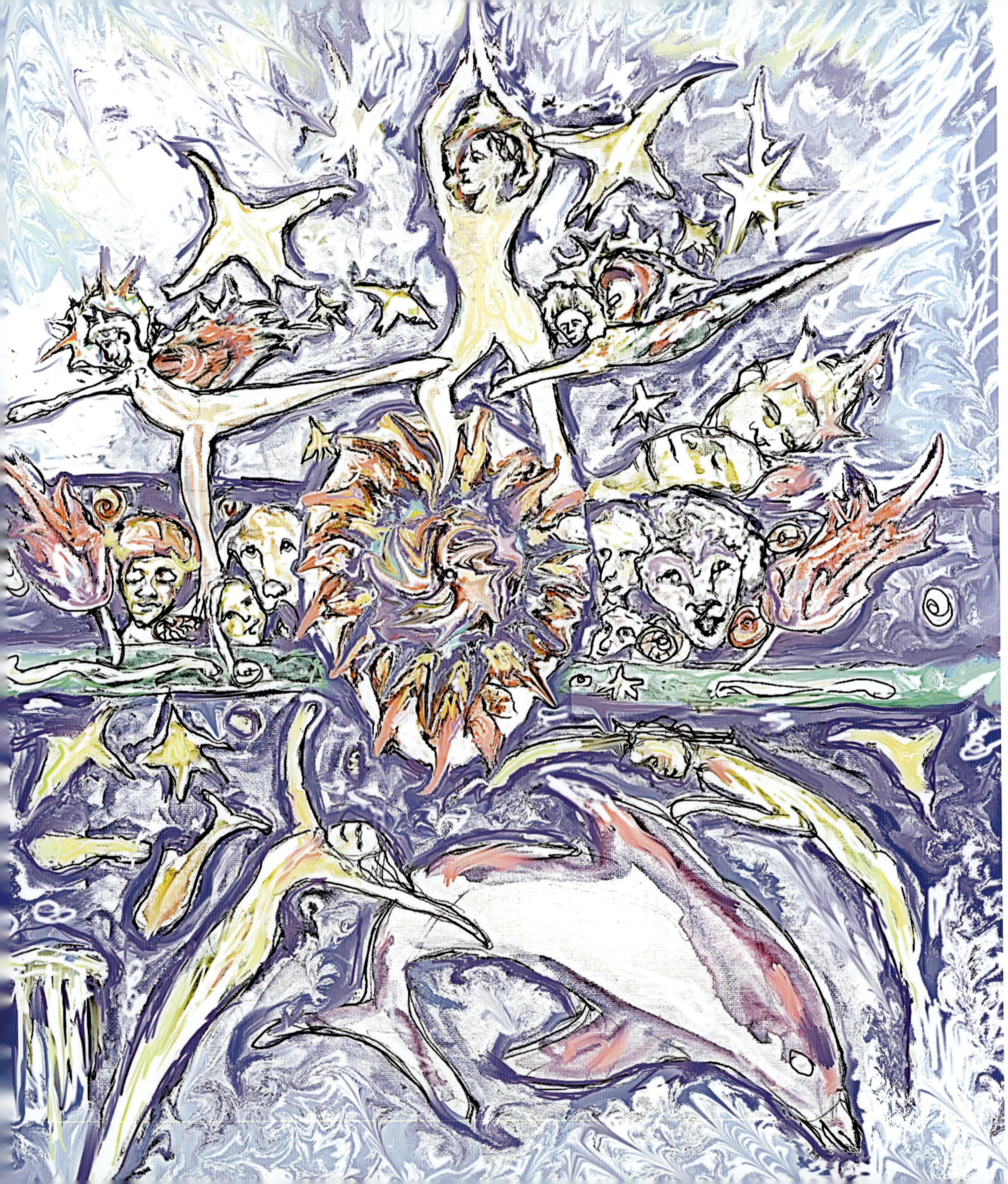

One Spirit loved the diversity it had beome. It was now...

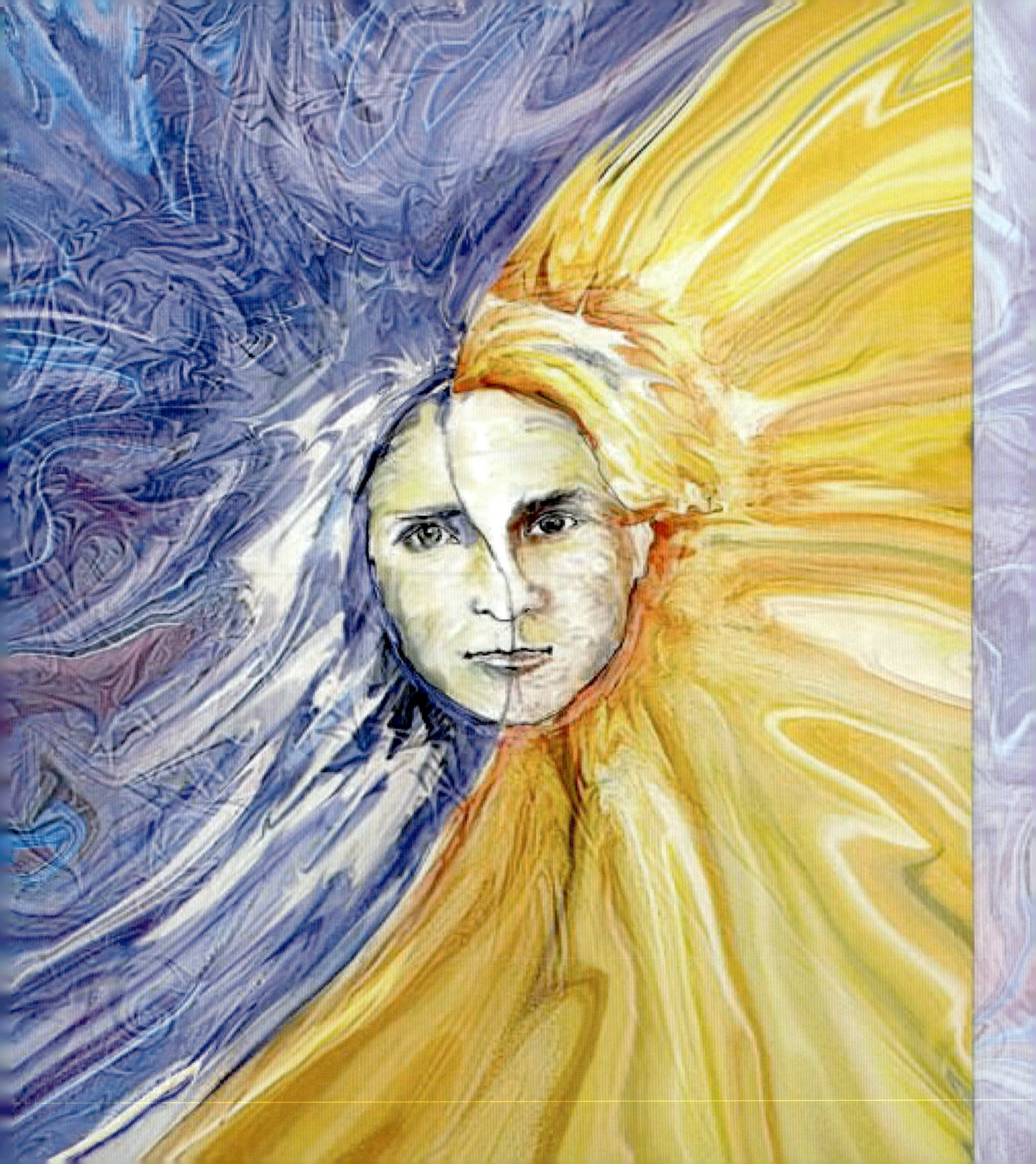

Male and female

human,

plant

and

animal,

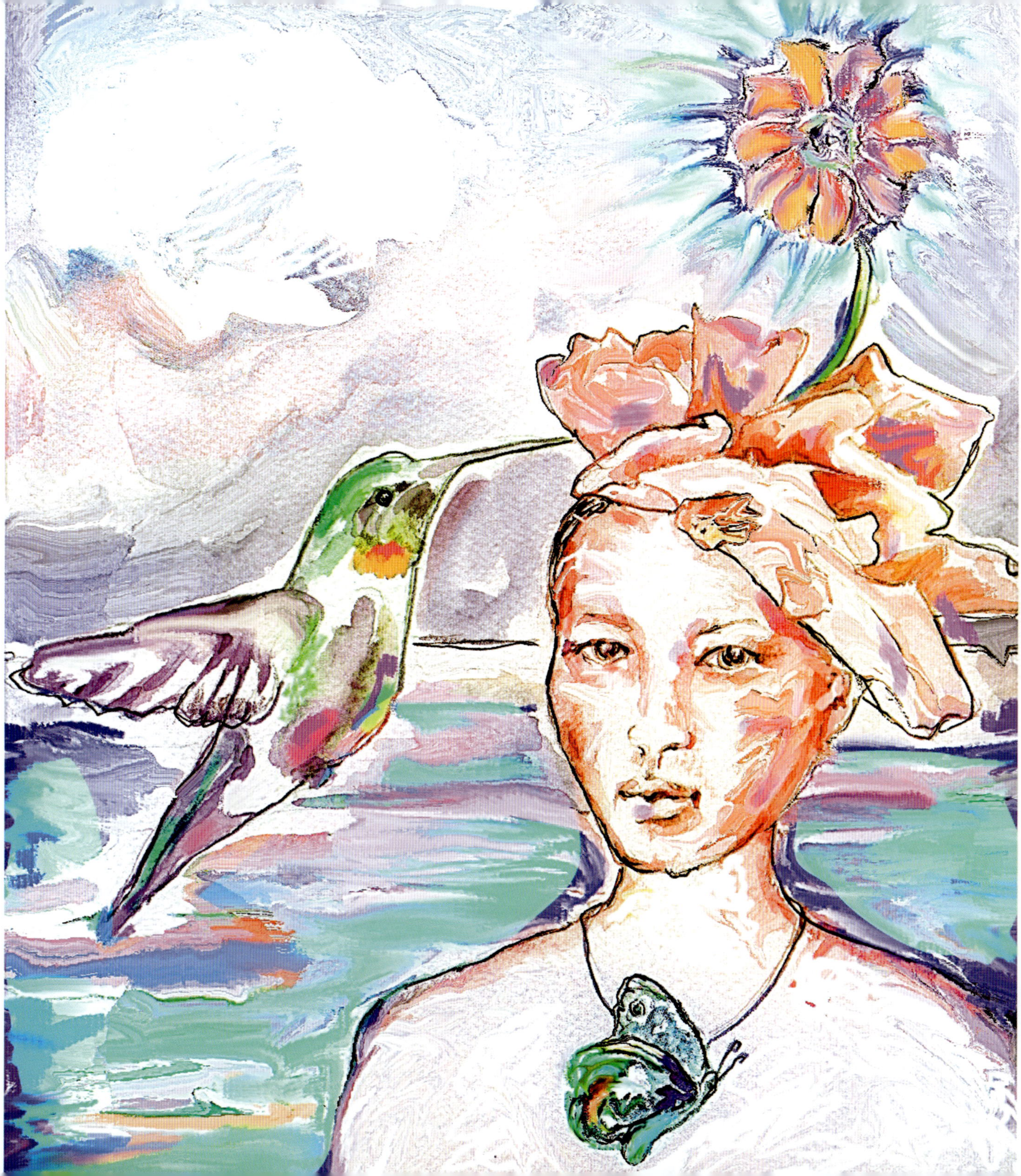

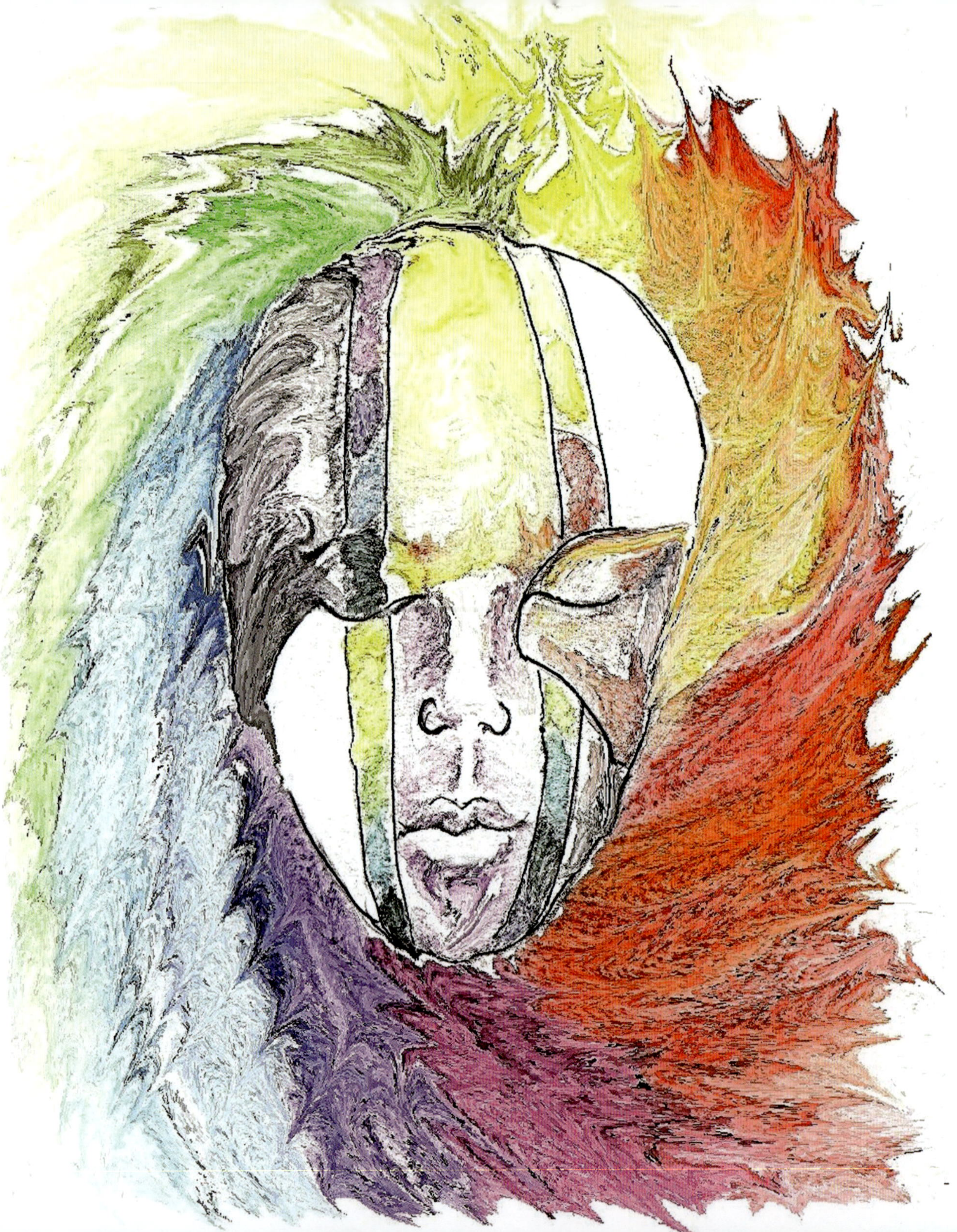

black,

white,

brown,

red and yellow,

gay and straight.

But always
One Spirit.

Just as lung cells
and skin cells
and blood cells
are one body.

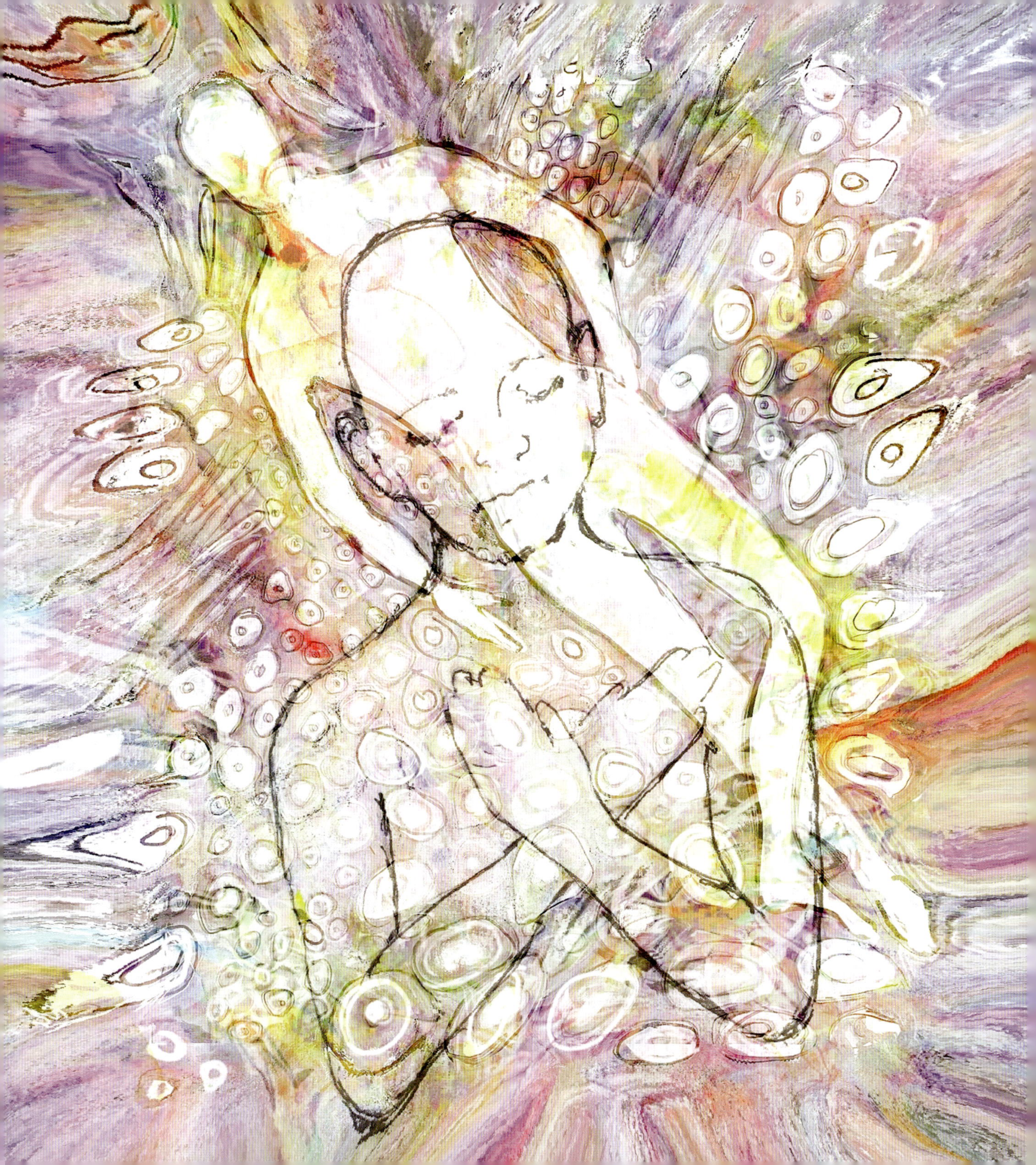

When the living beings died, their bodies passed back into the Earth.

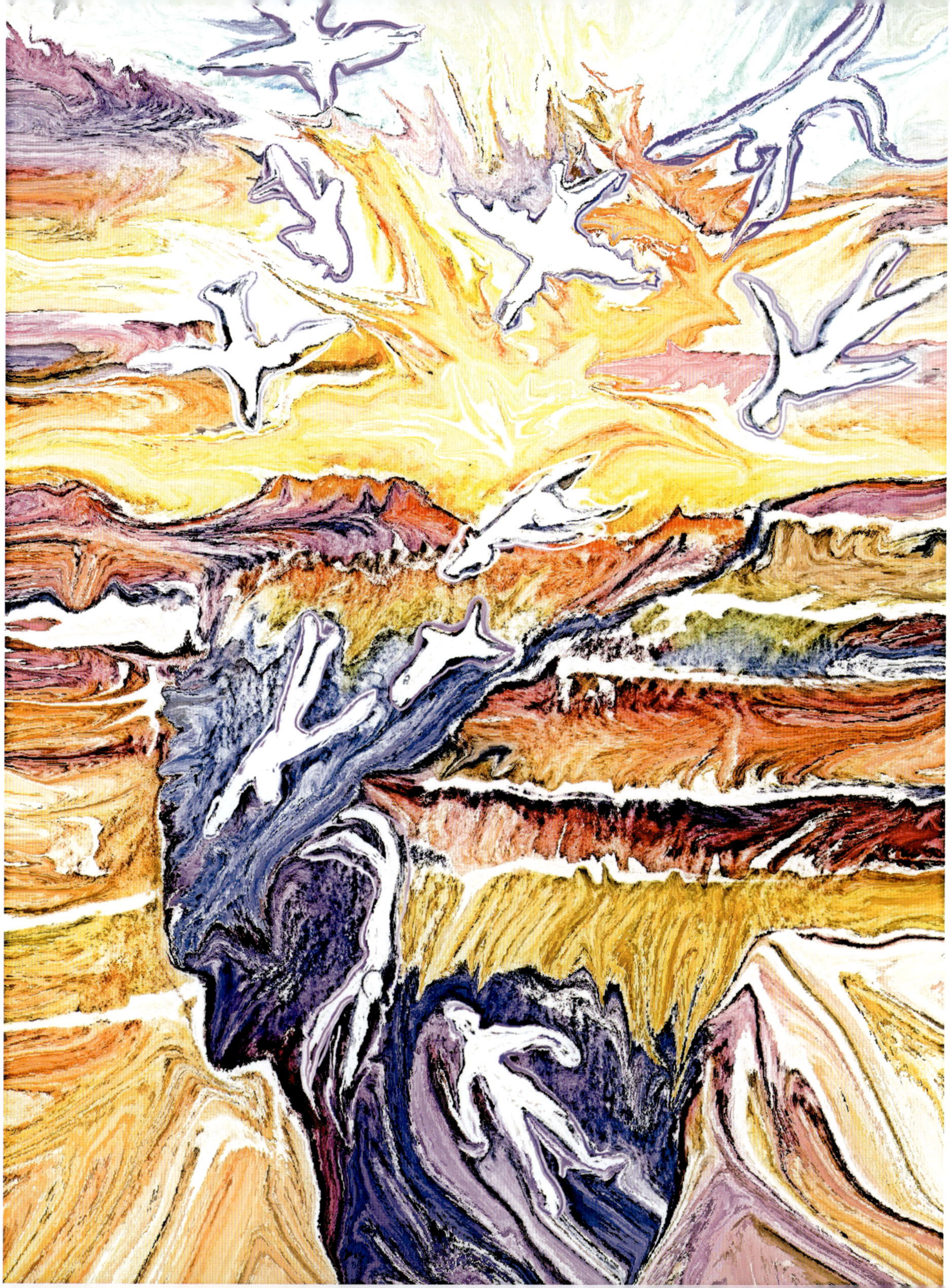

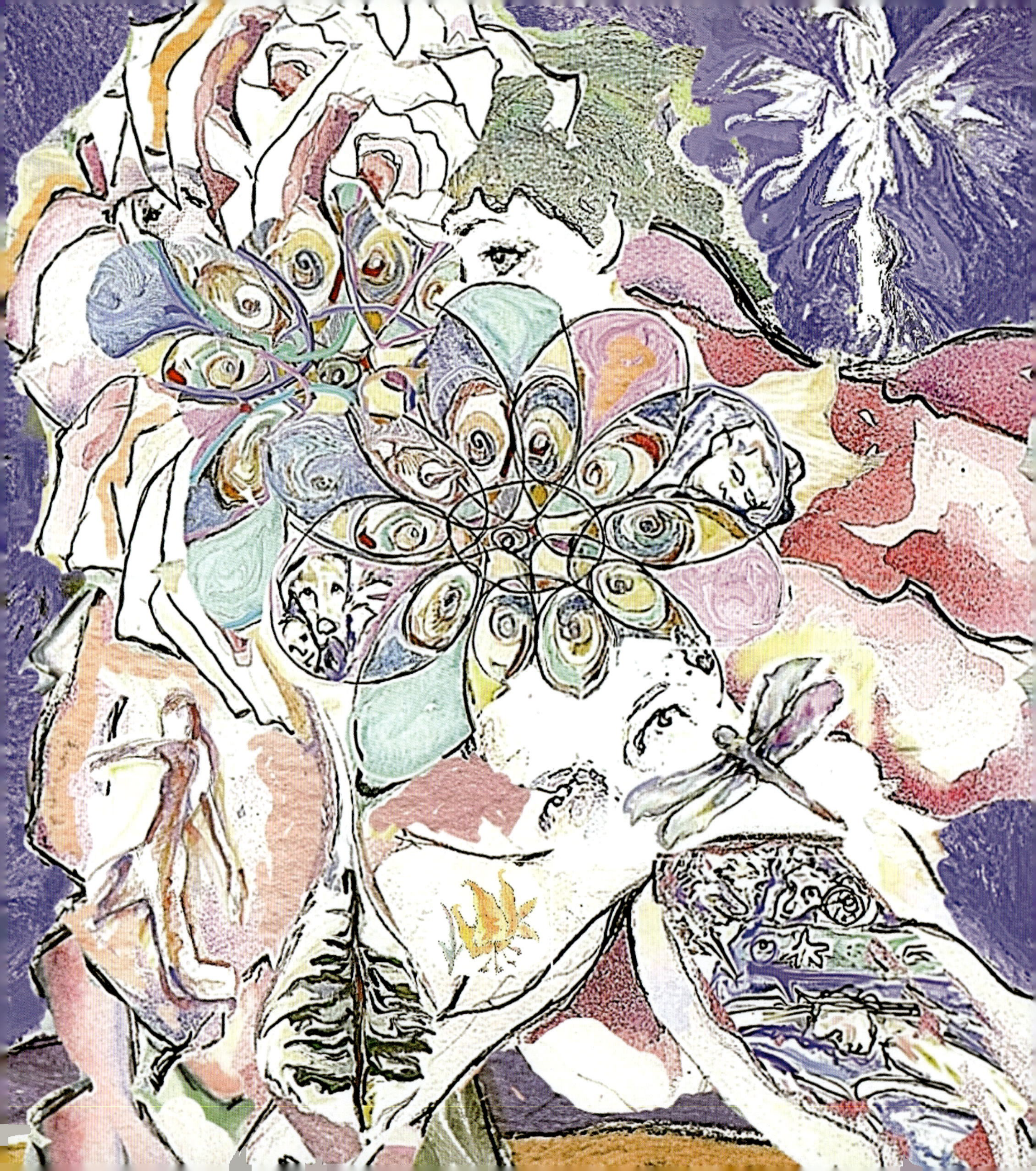

And the unique

awareness

they had developed

merged back into

One Spirit.

But One Spirit loved diversity

and playfulness so much,

that each awareness,

each person,

kept his or her own identity

upon return...

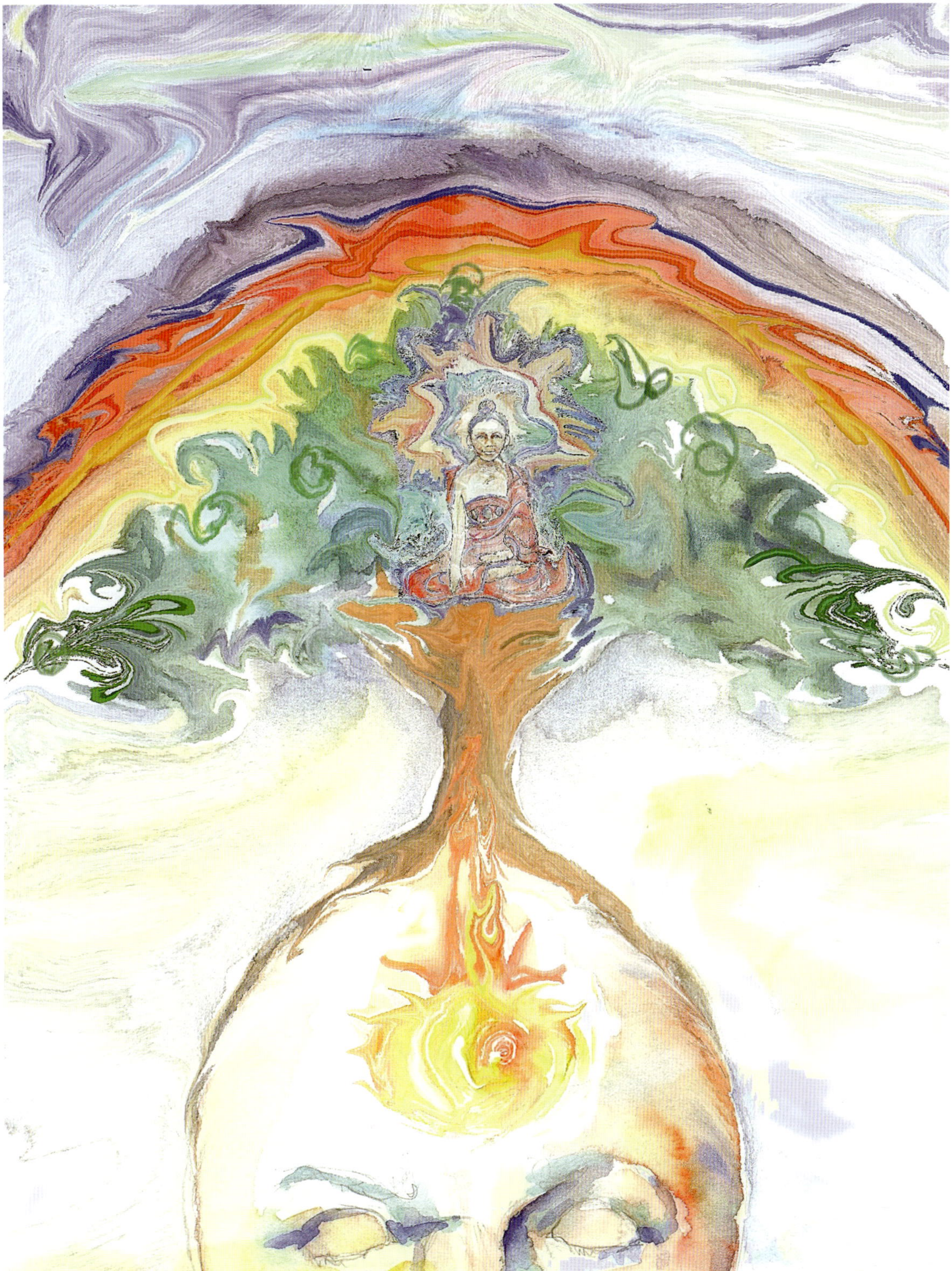

... after being a

man,

woman,

child,

plant

or

animal...

to One Spirit.

What

had

been created

through

differentiation...

the unique combination of emotions, idiosyncracies, thoughts, beliefs, talents, relationships ...

Did not

disappear

when the body

no longer

functioned.

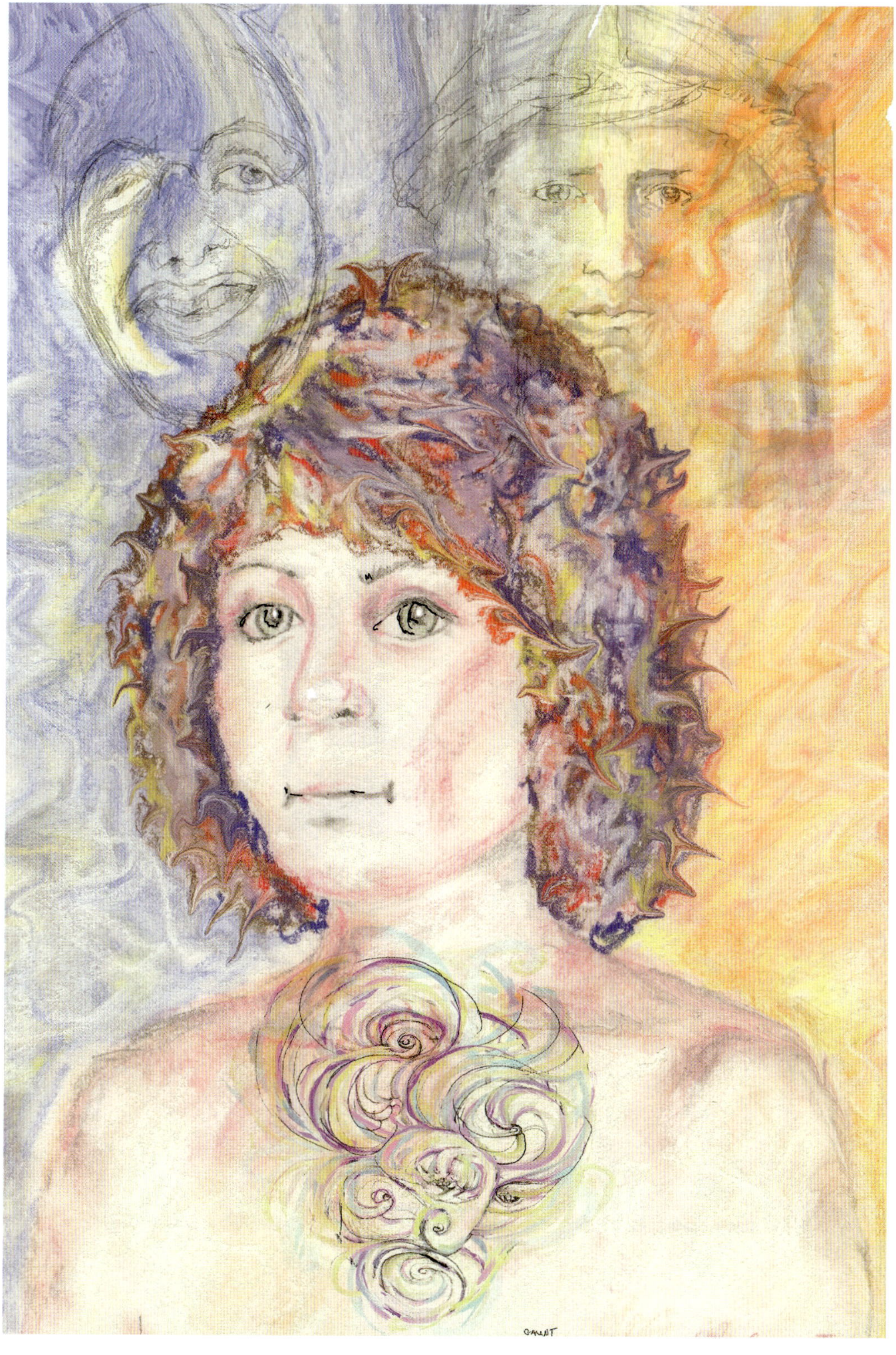

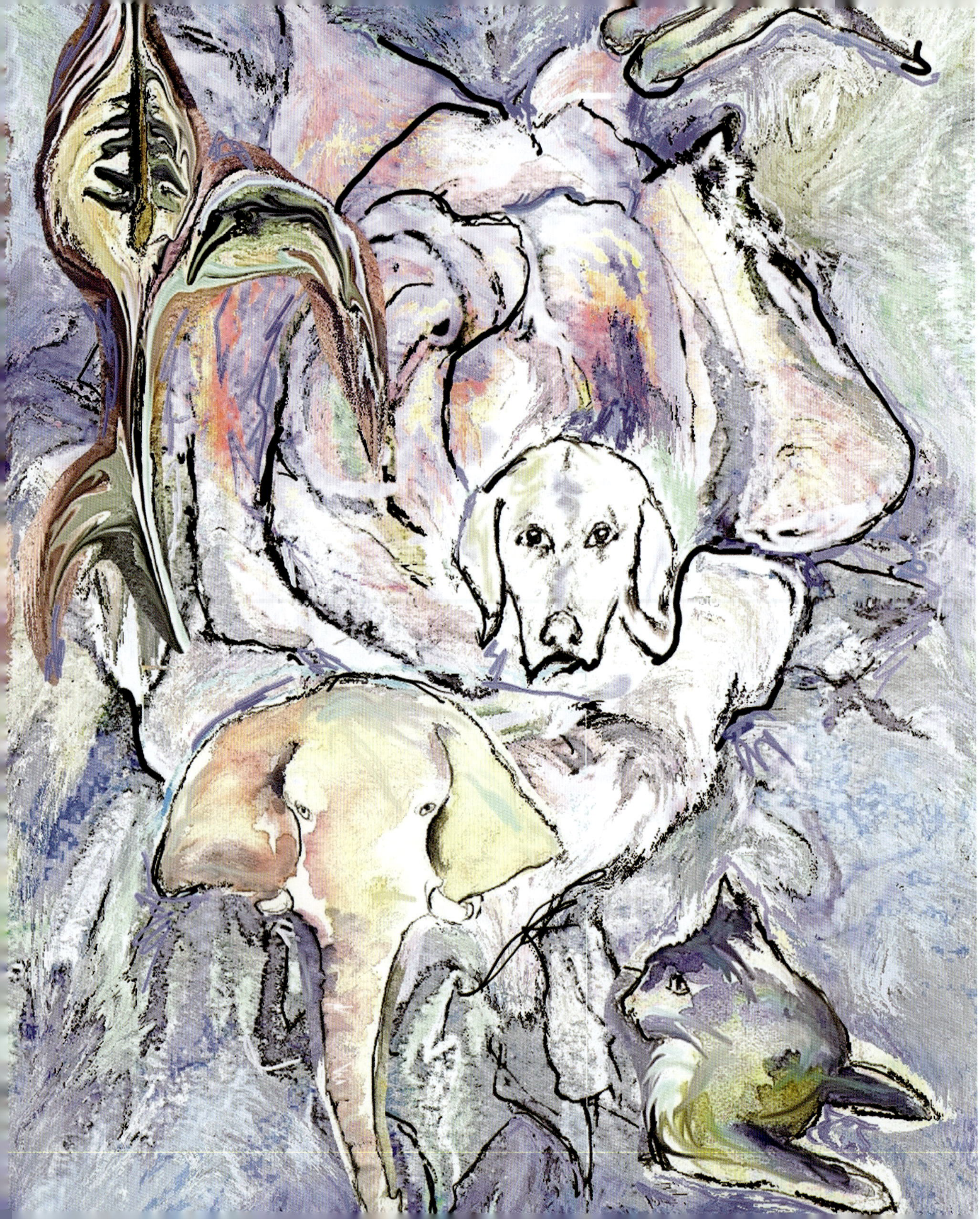

So One Spirit,

for all eternity,

was thrilled...

Not only

with the material

playground of diversity

on Earth

and in the Universe,

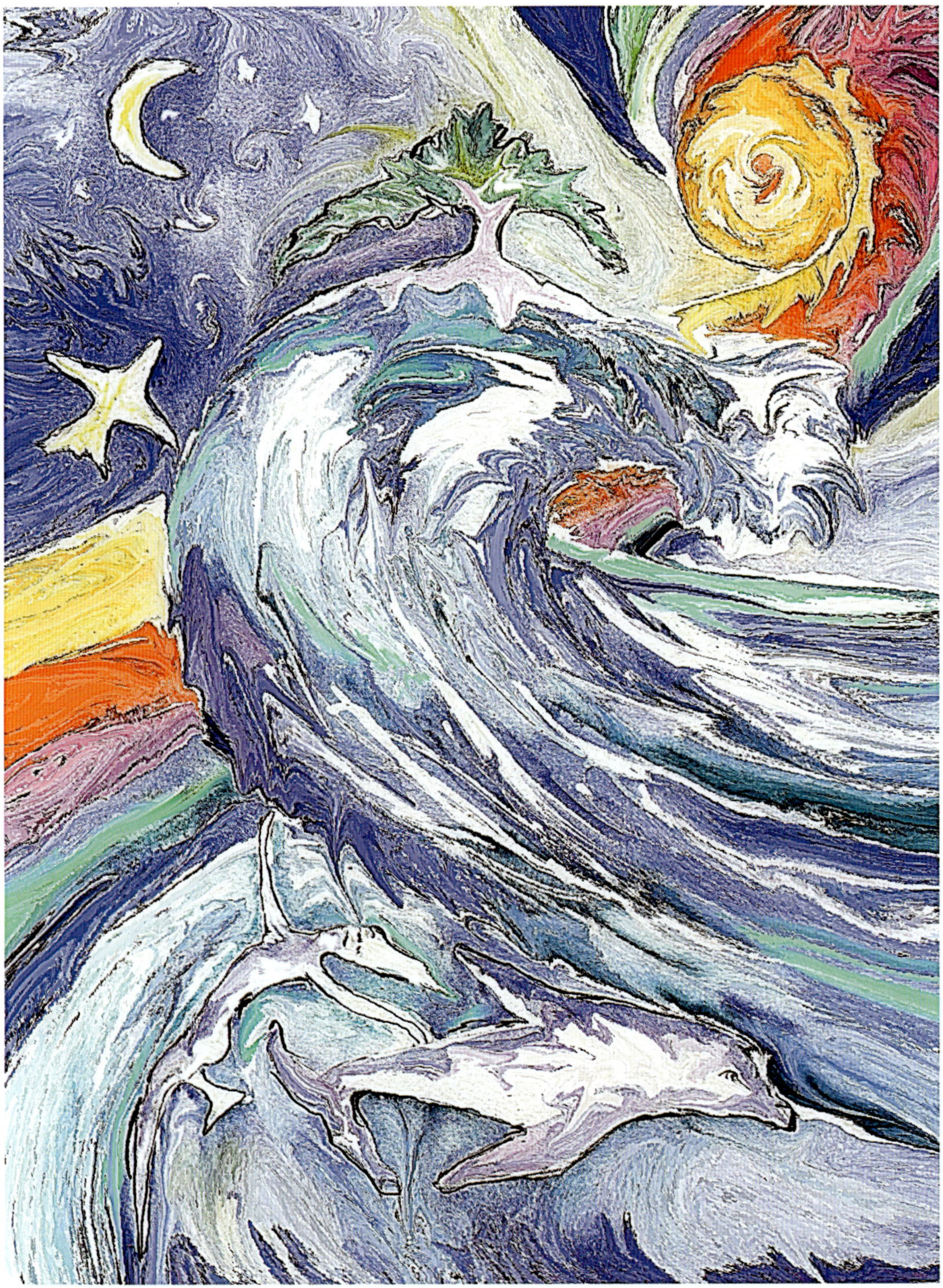

but with the intensely exciting spiritual interplay

of all the living beings who had ever existed.

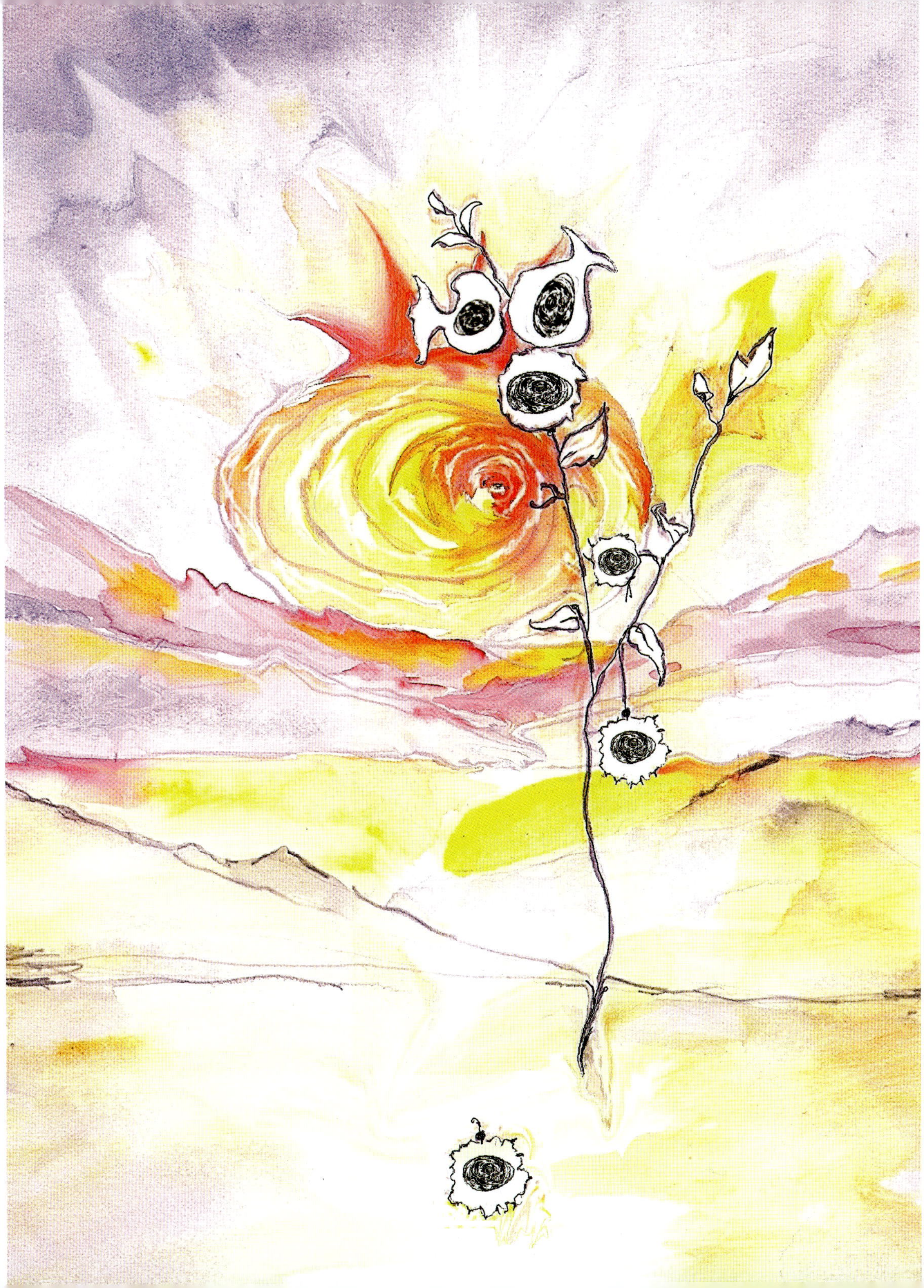

And
all
those
beings...

men, women, babies...

cats,

dogs...

elephants and dragon flies...

roses,

lilies and

redwood

trees,

took delight

in an infinity of

playfulness,

growth and love.

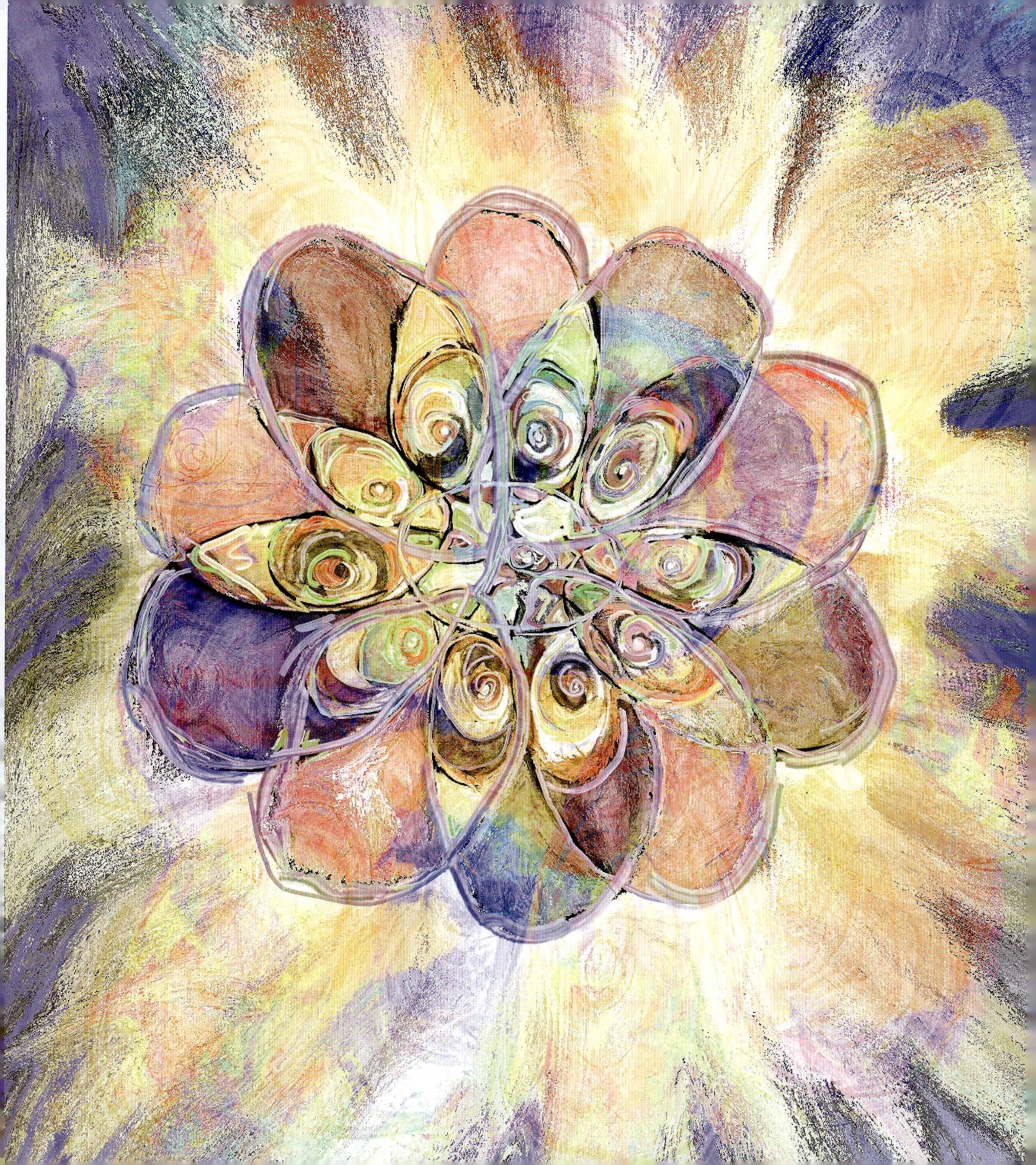